Living in Peace

KENNON L. CALLAHAN, PH.D.

The National Institute for Church Planning and Consultation
PMB 280, 381 Casa Linda Plaza
Dallas, Texas 75218

For information, contact Dr. Kennon L. Callahan, Ph.D.
The National Institute for Church Planning and Consultation
PMB 280, 381 Casa Linda Plaza, Dallas, Texas 75218

Library of Congress Cataloging in Publication Data
Library of Congress Control Number: 2013914151
CreateSpace Independent Publishing Platform
North Charleston, SC

Callahan, Ph.D., Kennon L.
Living in Peace.

1. Life. 2. Missions. 3. Leadership. 4. Peace   I. Title
    2013
ISBN: 1491088753
ISBN-13: 9781491088753

12   13   14   15   16   17

Table of Contents

Dedication

EILEEN BEATRICE ARTHUR CALLAHAN

Living in Peace is dedicated to my Mother.

She was five years old when Harry Arthur, her father, was killed in an oil rig tragedy near Sapulpa, Oklahoma. Her sister, Marion, was three. Her mother, Arta, in later life we called her Mimi, as our grandmother, and the two young girls had gone with their father to the oilfields of Oklahoma to seek their fortune.

Harry had become an excellent oil rig bit sharpener. Such an ability was greatly valued in the newly discovered oil fields of southern Oklahoma. They had gathered themselves up and traveled from their home in Lima, Ohio to faraway Sapulpa. They lived near an oil field, in a one room shack, with just almost enough of a roof over their heads.

In the earliest days, it was called Sapulpa Station because it was basically the junction of two railroads. Sapulpa was the Indian chief of the area. It was a rustic, early beginning town.

When Harry was killed, Arta, Eileen, and Marion returned to Lima, Ohio. There was nothing left for them in the oil fields. Eileen and Marion had always been close as sisters. With the passing of their father, they became even closer.

Years passed. They grew even closer.

Both married. Both enjoyed their beginning families. By 1942, Eileen had two sons, Ken and Dan, five and three. Marion had two daughters, Lynne and Nancy, four and two.

In October of 1942, during the war, Marion gave birth to her third daughter, Valerie. As she was leaving the hospital three days later, Marion got into the car, sat down, sighed, and died. An embolism. That was the possibility.

Mom, that day, became the mother of all five children, the newly born baby, Valerie, the two-year-old, Nancy, the four-year-old, Lynne, the three-year-old, my brother, Dan, and me, the five-year-old, Ken.

Mom was twenty-eight years old.

Mom had help from my grandmother, Mimi.

My Dad was fighting the war in the Pacific. The girls' father, Francis, was fighting the war in Europe. My grandmother, in her fifties, came on board to help Mom with the girls and with my younger brother and myself. We called my grandmother, Mimi. Mimi's sister, Aunt Bea, was a help as well.

We lived, for a time, on Myrtle Avenue. Mimi and the girls lived on the second floor of our triplex. A teacher rented the third floor apartment. Mom, my younger brother, and I lived on the first floor. It was a good arrangement.

Then, we moved to Third Street to be nearer the grade school. Here, Mom, my brother, and I lived on the second floor, and

Mimi and the three girls lived on the first floor. The war moved forward. Mom, Mimi, and Aunt Bea did well for the five children. Mostly, it was Mom and Mimi. And the five of us. We did well.

Dad and Uncle Francis came home from the war. We continued to help one another. We had become virtually one family. I still think of the three girls as my sisters.

Over the years that came and went, people in the town would say, again and again,

"That Mrs. Callahan is a saint. She took on all five children, the two of her own and the three of her sister's. She has done well by them."

She is among the most outstanding mothers I have ever known. Her grace and thoughtfulness, her gifted love and warm spirit, her gentle laughter and spirit of fun, her sense of peace and calm brought out the best in all of us.

Amidst the calamities of life, Mom had the gift of peace. With the difficulties and tragedies of life, she had a remarkable ability for living in peace.

She loved all five children. She loved my father. She loved the family. She lived a life of grace and peace.

This book is dedicated to her.

Kennon L. Callahan
August 11, 2013

Words of Appreciation

JULIE CALLAHAN

Living in Peace is advanced and improved by Julie Callahan.
We are best friends. We love one another.
On August 11, 2013, we celebrated our
fifty-seventh wedding anniversary.
God blesses us with grace and peace and
a wonderful life together.

Julie lives a life of peace.
She has taught me much about a spirit of peace and calm.
Her wonderful gift of peace is a wondrous blessing in my life.

She has contributed many helpful suggestions
to the final text of *Living in Peace*.

It is a better book for her improvements.
I am most grateful for her love,
for our life together,
and for her wise, thoughtful suggestions.

DORIS HOFFMAN

Doris is Julie's cousin.
They grew up near each other in Cuyahoga Falls, Ohio
where we five children lived.

Doris has had a distinguished career in research
and she has a gifted, remarkable calling in the field of music.

She has been gracious to serve as reader for *Living in Peace*.
Her wisdom, her encouraging spirit, and her precision of focus
have made this work an even more helpful, insightful work.

I am grateful to her for sharing excellent suggestions and good ideas.
Doris has a deep love for life, ministry, and music.
She brings much wisdom and experience for the benefit of this work.
She lives a life of peace.

RICHARD WORDEN

I want to thank Richard Worden for his friendship,
and for our amazing four research trips together.
The first was to the Antarctic, Argentina, and Chile.
The second research trip was to Turkey, Greece, Italy, and Spain.
The third research trip was to Norway, Denmark, Sweden,
Finland, Estonia, Germany, and Russia.

Our fourth research trip, in June of 2013,
has been to the Svalbard Islands.
Our itinerary took us to these ports of call: Washington, D. C. to
Amsterdam, flight, Board Celebrity Constellation, At Sea, Arctic
Circle Crossing, Leknes (Lofoten) Norway, Arctic Circle Cruise,
Longyearbyen Norway, Arctic Circle Cruise, Honningsvag Nor-
way, Arctic Circle Crossing, Molde Norway, Bergen Norway, At
Sea, Dock in Amsterdam, and Amsterdam to Washington, D. C.,
flight. We sailed for 3,613.21 Nautical Miles.
It was an amazing trip.

Our current research interests are in both cultural
archaeology and in human behavior.

His encouraging spirit, his wisdom, and his thoughtful comments
have made this book an even more helpful and insightful work.
He lives a life of peace.

It was during this trip that the content and structure of
Living in Peace came into being.

CREATESPACE

I am grateful to CreateSpace
and the impressive staff of persons who have
nurtured this work to full publication.
I have enjoyed our work together.
Our work on *Living in Grace*, our first book together,
moved very well.
Our work on this book has flowed remarkably well. It has been a
joy to work with them. Of course,
I take full responsibility for the final book.

For this book, *Living in Peace*, I want to especially thank
Lauren Cooley, who has served as team leader, Becca Curtis,
who has provided design services, and Ashley Strosnider,
who has provided promotional text services.
They are a fantastic team, and I have greatly
enjoyed working with them.

Many, many people – the persons who
participated in these events,
the special reader team who helped me with the book,
and the publisher's staff - bring this book to you.

May you enjoy and benefit from *Living in Peace*.

Beginnings

BE AT PEACE

These are gentle words. These are encouraging words. They whisper. They speak softly. They murmur with grace. They bring a sense of calm. We are content. We have a sense of balance and satisfaction. Life is good. We are at peace.

Across the years, I have said these words, "Be at peace," many, many times. For me, these words are a form of blessing. I share these words with an encouraging spirit. These words encourage a spirit of calm, of quiet contentment, of gentle serenity. They encourage a relaxed stillness. They encourage a simple, gentle grace and peace.

We search for peace. We long for and yearn for peace. Amidst the swirl and fury, the thunder and the lighting all around us, we want peace.

We search for roots, place, and belonging. We search for individuality and community. We search for meaning. We search for hope. We search for creativity and stability. We search for ways beyond calamity. We search for new good surprises. We search for grace.

We search for peace.

In life, we experience moments of anxiety and fear, anger and rage, upsetness and upheaval, calamity and catastrophe, despair and sadness. We experience war and disaster, drought and fire, tragedy and misfortune. We know sickness and death.

And, we experience moments of surprise and delight, joy and wonder, laughter and fun, gladness and happiness. We know birthings and growings, new discoveries and innovations. Life is a mix of moments.

A few persons may not long for peace.

They long for a fight. They long to express their anger, their fear, their sense of betrayal, their panic of abandonment, their love of a fight. They are gloomy and grumpy. A few persons seem to carry a grudge. They remember unhappy, sad, and bitter times. They seethe and resent, bemoan and complain.

Yet, underneath all of these lesser possibilities, there may be a deep-seated, intuitive longing for peace. God gives to us the longing for peace. For the moment, a few persons may long to fight. Most persons yearn for moments of peace.

Peace sings. The melody of peace is gentle and stirring. Peace is happy and joyful, not solemn and serious. Sweet, sweet peace blesses our days with songs of grace. We are cheerful and contented. We are calm. We are at peace.

Peace smiles. Peace laughs. Peace leaps with joy. Peace has fun. Peace is vibrant and ecstatic. Peace brings the joy of living.

In times of tragedy and sadness, peace cries. Peace surrounds us with succor and solace, comfort and consolation. The security of peace surrounds us with a calm stillness. We are encouraged to be at peace, with confidence and assurance in the grace of God.

Peace and prayer are good friends. Peace and mercy are good friends. Peace and forgiveness are good friends. When we share prayer, mercy, and forgiveness, we live in peace.

Peace and pace are good friends.

Live life at a pace that is comfortable for you. For solid marathon runners, the comfortable pace is slow and steady, regular and routine. For excellent sprinters, the comfortable pace is short-term, highly intensive, near the time at hand. Both are at peace with the pace that is comfortable with them. Find the pace that matches with you and be at peace.

Peace is happy. Peace is glad. Peace is never sad. Peace is never gloomy. Peace is never angry. Peace is never depressed.

God blesses us with moments of peace and calm.

Peace-filled events change our lives and shape our destinies. Events are decisive when they are filled with grace and peace.

Our lives are filled with everyday, ordinary happenings. We live and move and have our being amidst the regular, routine events of life. We get up. We dress. We go to work. We tend to chores around the house. We enjoy meals.

We talk and share with one another. We worry. We wonder. We storm. We shout. We are glad. We are sad. We laugh. We cry. We play. We love. We go to sleep. We get up.

We live life day-to-day, week-to-week, season-to-season, year-to-year, hardly noticing as the years come and go. We experience people, we experience events, we remember old friends, we discover new friends, we practice old habits, and we turn up new possibilities. Mostly, we use our time well.

Amidst the everyday, ordinary events of life, we experience peace-filled events that change our lives and shape our destinies. We experience the grace and peace of God in these events.

Be at peace.

PEACE COMES

Peace is a gift we receive.

Peace is not our own doing. We do not manufacture peace. We do not fabricate and construct peace. We do not make peace happen. Peace does not well up from within us. We are not the cause of peace. We do not instigate peace.

God gives moments of peace to us. We are blessed with the grace and peace of God. In generous and gracious ways, God shares the gifts of grace and peace with us.

We experience events of grace and moments of peace.

It is not as though we experience peace all of the time.

We experience moments of fear and anxiety, anger and rage, despair and disappointment, sadness and calamity. Life is filled with a rich range of moments and events. Some are happy. Some are sad. Some are filled with tension. Some are filled with peace.

The art is to experience more moments of peace and calm and fewer events of tension and strain.

Living in Peace will help. The book describes moments of peace, peace filled events, which have encouraged many people to live their lives filled with moments of peace and contentment.

Be at peace. Peace comes.

PEACE AND PROGRESS

Peace and progress are good friends.

Some of us, in an earlier time, learned a compulsive, addictive, perfectionism. It has served us, from one perspective, well. We have gotten where we are, we have achieved and accomplished what we have because of our compulsive, addictive, perfectionism. We have been tense and tight, nervous and anxious, driven and obsessed. And, it has worked. Sort of.

It has also been a disaster.

A pattern of compulsive, addictive, perfectionism creates a compulsive, addictive, perfectionism toward peace. It creates the pervasive notion that peace must be present all of the time, in full measure, one hundred percent. Always present. Never absent. A full measure of peace. But, with a strident, demanding, compulsive expectation for peace, there is no peace.

The art is to be at peace about peace. The art is progress, not perfection. The art is to relax and look for moments of peace, not peace all of the time. The art is to receive, graciously and generously, the moments of peace with which God blesses us.

When we strive, we do not thrive. When we are at peace, we thrive. When we try hard to be at peace, we become tense and tight, nervous and anxious. We become preoccupied with peace. We become insistent on peace all of the time,

Be at peace much of the time, or some of the time, or now and then. But do not strive for peace all of the time. To strive for peace all of the time is to have peace none of the time. When we strive - hear the word, "*strive*" - for peace all of the time, we end up getting peace none of the time.

We want to be at peace about moments of peace. We can have the confidence and assurance that God blesses us with moments of peace. God is generous with the blessings of grace and peace.

Grace and peace are good friends. Where there is grace, there is peace. Where there is peace, there is grace. Be at peace.

Be at peace. Peace comes. Peace and progress are good friends.

POSSIBILITIES FOR PEACE

God gives us moments of peace. God gives us persons from whom we learn about peace. These persons have helped me learn much about peace in our lives. Enjoy discovering these persons and the possibilities they give you for experiencing moments of peace in your life.

We find peace not by looking for peace. Oh, to some extent, we may. Mostly, we find peace as a result of looking for something else. Peace is the plus, the bonus.

Enjoy coming o know these persons. Enjoy these events. Be at peace.

> Eunice
> Gene, Charles, Ken
> Opal
> Grandma Ida and Kate
> Mom, Mimi, Aunt Bea
> St. John's
> Dorothy
> Grand Children
> Orville
> Julie and Ken

These are real-life events. These are real-life persons. These are decisive events that have helped me understand the nature of peace. I have shared these events just as they happened, without embellishment. There are no added "features." These events took place just as I have told them.

These events have taken on the strength of being parables because each of these events is filled with the grace and peace of God. Those of us who participated in each of these events experienced the grace and peace of God.

In the years come and gone, as I have shared these events, many, many people, in fresh, new ways, have experienced the peace of God in their own lives. These events have become parables of peace.

As you read each of these events, think of moments in your life....

of grace and compassion....

of fun, with joy and wonder....

of peace and calm....

Claim these moments. Live in grace. Live in peace. Have fun, with the joy and the wonder of life. Experience the grace and peace of God.

Be at peace. Peace comes. Peace and progress are good friends.
Live these possibilities for peace.

Eunice and Mrs. Perkins

I invite you to be kind with Eunice.

"Ken, come quick. Something has happened with Eunice."

Late that Saturday morning, Mrs. Perkins called.

There was distress and anguish, panic and pain in her voice. Mrs. Perkins had never called in that urgent, desperate way before.

I went quickly. I had had my own concerns for her sister, Eunice.

I always called Mrs. Perkins by her formal name. She is "Mrs. Perkins." She has a gentle, kind nature. She is quiet and peaceful, warm and generous. Her gracious dignity and thoughtful manner, her poise and goodness were wonderful gifts of grace.

The desperation of her plea caused me to go quickly.

When I got to Mrs. Perkins' home, she was outside on the porch, anxious, troubled, worried, pacing up and down.

Ordinarily, she would have been inside. I would have rung the doorbell. She would have come to the door, opened the door, and invited me in. We would have had tea or coffee, a pleasant visit, and I would have left.

This time she was outside, on the porch. She ran to greet me, throwing her arms around me.

"Oh, Ken, something has happened with Eunice. I don't know what to do."

That spring, Mrs. Perkins and I had stood day-by-day at Tom's hospital bedside. He was gravely ill, lingered long, and, finally, passed away. I shared the funeral service with Mrs. Perkins and some of her friends.

Three days later, Mrs. Perkins and I had gone back out to the cemetery and stood by Tom's grave and had prayers with one another, with Tom, and with God.

It was a tough time for Mrs. Perkins. She and Tom had met in grade school, grown up together, become good friends, fell in love, married, and lived a long, wonderful, devoted life together. They were good partners. He was gone. It was a tough time for her.

Eunice was Mrs. Perkins' maiden sister, born on the old homestead in Nearly Nowhere, in a neighboring state. She had grown up on the old homestead. She had lived her whole life there. She had never been anywhere. She was shy and bashful, and content to live on the old homestead.

On the occasion of Tom's death, Eunice did what good sisters do. She gathered up all her courage and left the world she knew and came to the big city to spend a few weeks with her good sister, so Mrs. Perkins would not be by herself during the day. She would have company at each meal. She would not feel alone as she passed Tom's favorite chair, and, in her mind, still saw him sitting there.

And, in the evening when Mrs. Perkins went to bed, she would know there was someone in the house with her. She would not be alone. She would have company.

Mrs. Perkins and Eunice had come to church. I had been by the home several times. Eunice and I had become friends.

In July, Eunice was still there. She lingered longer than she had ordinarily planned.

Eunice could see that it was a hard time for her sister. She had stayed.

Toward the end of July, I began to have my own concerns for Eunice. You could almost see a tense tightness appear on her face, a look of scared panic began to creep into her eyes.

So that Saturday morning in early August when the phone call came, I went quickly.

Mrs. Perkins explained she had been in the kitchen early that morning fixing breakfast.

Eunice was coming and leaving, coming and leaving, coming and leaving the kitchen. Mrs. Perkins simply assumed that Eunice was doing some things around the house, helping with the chores.

When Mrs. Perkins had breakfast ready, she called Eunice.

Eunice did not come.

Mrs. Perkins called again. Then, she went hunting for Eunice. She could not find her. She looked all through the house. Finally, she found her.

This is where I invite you to be kind with Eunice.

Mrs. Perkins found Eunice in the bathroom.

For whatever reason, early that morning it had come to Eunice, she felt led to know this was the day, Saturday, to wash the clothes. For whatever reason, she was drawn to washing the clothes – it would be the best place, she thought - in the bath tub, not in the washing machine. She did not know how to run her sister's washing machine. At home, Eunice used a large wash tub. The bath tub would work.

Eunice gathered up all the clothes she could find around the house and put them in the bath tub. She turned the water on, and put in the soap.

In her coming and leaving the kitchen, Eunice went into the pantry and gathered whatever strange array of condiments she could find on the shelves and brought them and dumped them in the bath tub. Cereal, corn syrup, pickles, jam, olives – just whatever was on the shelves. She came in, picked them up, carried them to the bathroom, opened them, and dumped them into that ungodly mess in the bath tub.

When Mrs. Perkins found her beloved sister, Eunice was stirring the ungodly mess with the upside-down handle of a broom.

Mrs. Perkins was understandably upset. They were mostly her clothes in that mess. Eunice had not brought that many clothes with her.

Mrs. Perkins naturally objected to what her good sister, Eunice, was doing. Mrs. Perkins almost held the words in check. Later, she said she wished she had. She almost contained herself. She almost kept her resolve.

Then, the words came tumbling out. The hospital. The funeral. The graveside. The loneliness. Missing Tom. Oh, missing Tom. The heat of the summer. Everything. Now this.

Eunice and Mrs. Perkins exchanged a mixture of hurried, spilling over, upsetting, angry words.

This reminded Eunice she had forgotten to get the pillowcases and the bed sheets. She went and got them off the beds and dumped them into the ungodly mess in the bath tub.

Even two sisters who dearly love one another, who are simply trying to help one another through this life's pilgrimage as best they can, have been known to exchange words and gently tussle, shove, and push in a hallway on a Saturday morning.

All the stresses and strains of Tom's illness and death and Eunice's weeks in that strange, big city had been too much. With the sharp exchange of words, and the tussling, shoving, and pushing, Eunice went to the kitchen to find the largest butcher knife she could lay her hands on, so she could hold her sister at bay, while she did what she felt she had been called to do.

Seeing the large butcher knife pointed her way, that's when Mrs. Perkins had gone to the phone and called me.

In the brief time it took me to get there, some further words were exchanged, more heated this time. The result was that Eunice had slashed in two sets of curtains with the butcher knife and was working on the sofa in the living room. This was why Mrs. Perkins was standing outside on the porch.

It is amazing to me what kind of help you cannot get, even living in a big city, on a Saturday morning. We called the police department, and they said they would come just as soon as she stabbed one of us. She hadn't done anything – yet.

Well, Mrs. Perkins and I drew a line in the sand, and we both stood on one side of the line and we talked it over and wondered who would step over the line and volunteer to be the one to be stabbed. Neither of us stepped across the line.

We called the county mental health association. We got a pleasant, cheerful, charming voice on the telephone. It was an answering machine, informing us that the offices would be open at 9:00 A.M. on Monday and to please call back then. Right then, on that Saturday, Monday morning at nine o'clock looked like a long time away.

We called the nearby hospital. Could they help? "Sure," they said, "bring her over." The "bringing her over" part was the stumbling block. That did not look like something we were going to be able to do right then.

We did what good family do.

We called the brother and the nephew in Nearly Nowhere, and we held the fort for three long, long, long hours, as they drove down in their car. A better way to say it would be "as they flew down in their car." It is a four-hour trip for anyone driving really fast. They did the trip in three hours.

It is amazing what family do when someone in the clan is in trouble.

Then, when they got there, we did what good family do.

We stood around in the front yard, the brother, the nephew, Mrs. Perkins, and I, talking, wondering what we could do now. Finally, we came up with the idea that maybe Eunice would be better at home.

"Let's take Eunice home."

When that idea found common agreement, the brother and the nephew looked at me and said, "Would you go with us?

I said, "I don't see how I could. It is now late Saturday afternoon, and we have three worship services on Sunday morning, 8:00, 9:30, and 11:00. I don't see how I could hardly get back for the 8:00 o'clock service."

The brother said, "Don't worry. There is a mail plane at 2:00 A.M. out of the nearby airport. We will see you are on that plane."

It was amazing to me, when I said yes I would go with them, how quickly the brother and the nephew jumped into the front seats of the car, saying, "I'm sure you prefer to ride in the back seat with Eunice."

I said to Eunice, "Eunice, we're heading home. Give your sister a hug and a kiss. It's been a good visit. You have helped greatly. We're heading home. Lay the butcher knife on the porch. We'll leave it behind. It belongs to your sister. Give her a hug and a kiss."

She did.

I helped Eunice into the car, closed the door, and walked, with fear and trembling, around the back of the car to get to my side. I had not even gotten my door fully closed on my side of the car before we were heading out of the drive to the old homestead in Nearly Nowhere.

We did take four hours on the trip back.

It was four long, long, long, long hours in the back seat of the car on the way to Nearly Nowhere with Eunice. There were tears and sorrow, upsetness and anger. There was sullen silence. Words of recrimination. Words of regret. There was quiet talk. Some laughter. Gentle conversation.

Eunice taught me an extraordinary lesson that day.

You could almost see it as we got near familiar places and faces. You could almost see the tense tightness relax from her face. As we turned down the old dirt road – more dirt than road – leading to the old homestead, you could almost see the look of scared panic recede from her eyes.

We pulled up in the front yard – more dirt than yard – of the old homestead. I went around the car, opened the door, and helped Eunice out.

I said, "Eunice, we are home."

As best one can be, Eunice was virtually herself again.

Yes, we had invested late Saturday morning, early Saturday afternoon, and four hours in the back seat of a car on the way home. Yes, considerable time had passed.

And Eunice was home. There was about her a quiet contentment and gentle peace.

The clinical terms are societal dislocation and psychological disorientation. The busy, bustling, big city with its fast pace and strange ways had simply gotten to Eunice.

The lack of familiar faces and places had left her askew and lost.

Eunice taught me that day that when we find home, we find peace.

Bizarre events happen in the best of families. Now, it was not bizarre to put the clothes in the bath tub. That was how Eunice washed clothes in the old home stead, in a wash tub. And Saturday morning was the time to wash the clothes.

The bizarre part was the dumping of all the condiments, cereals, pickles, milk, orange juice, and on and on into the bath tub.

This was the strange and bizarre behavior that was Eunice's way of telling us she was in trouble. She could no longer sense where she was or who she was. She was coming undone.

The massive city had crushed in upon Eunice. The bigness and the busyness of the city contributed to her societal disorientation. She knew how to live in the old homestead, but the speed and pace, the crowdedness and confusion of the big city became more than she could handle.

The hardly knowing anyone, the bewilderment, the bafflement of the strange surroundings contributed to her psychological disorientation. She could not quite figure out who she was or where she was anymore. That morning, Eunice had been shouting out that it was more than she could take. She needed to be home.

We all have our fair share of psychological disorientation and societal dislocation. In our time, the pace is fast and furious. Stress is high. We see our fair share of bizarre events, even in the best of families.

For Eunice, home is peace. Peace is home.

Find home. You will find peace.

"Home" is not found among yelling and shouting, anger and confusion, disarray and disaster. "Home" is not found among bitterness and hostility, hate and resentment. "Home" is not found among lamenting and complaining.

For most of us, our search is for roots, place, belonging, friends, and family, where we discover grace and compassion, contentment and peace.

When we find home, we are at peace.

16

Gene, Charles, Ken

One year, with much enthusiasm, three good friends, Gene, Charles, and Ken, decided we would take 35 mm slide pictures of all the work and mission happening among our congregation across the coming months.

Thereby, during the stewardship campaign of the following October, we would have the best three-screen, three slide projector, multimedia with background music presentation of the mission of our congregation there had ever been.

With much enthusiasm, three cameras went busily "click, click, click" for many months. We had great fun. Our enthusiasm stirred. We took more pictures.

That fall, before the stewardship campaign, we gathered again, with much enthusiasm, at the corner drugstore with all of our little metal containers of film to have them developed. Historical note. In this earlier time, this was the way pictures were taken and developed.

The druggist was delighted to see us. He could see early retirement. The condominium in Florida was at last at hand. When the druggist told us how much it was going to cost to develop all those little metal containers of film, our enthusiasm sagged and slowly, sadly, solemnly nose-dived.

We knew we were not that good at tunneling. It would take a tunnel to Fort Knox to acquire some of the gold to pay for developing all those little metal containers of film. In our joyful enthusiasm, we had failed to mark which little metal containers had which pictures. In our carefree enthusiasm, it had been for us an all-or-nothing project.

Forlorn, dejected, despondent, we headed for the door to puzzle our next move. As we were nearing the door, the druggist hollered out, "Wait. I almost forgot. Eastman Kodak has just come out with self-developing kits. For a fraction of the cost, in the privacy of your own home, you can develop the film yourselves."

Our enthusiasm soared!

Gene, Charles, and Ken have been known to be drawn to new ventures and new projects. This would be even better than we had thought. With our enthusiasm towering, we each bought a chemical kit and a developing tank.

Loaded down with our bundles and packages, we headed, once again, to the door. As we were almost at the door, the druggist hollered out, "Wait. I almost forgot to tell you. You must get the film from the little metal container into the developing tank without exposing the film to a single ray of light."

"Once, you get the film on the spool, put the spool into the developing tank, fasten the lid securely on the tank, then you can take the developing tank to the kitchen, with the lights on, pour the chemicals, and develop the film. This is so new a product I don't know quite how to tell you how to get the film from the little metal container into the developing tank without exposing the film to a single ray of light."

Still, with renewed enthusiasm, confident we could figure something out, we headed to the door. We thought one or all of us could puzzle it through.

A couple of days later, my lifelong, good friend, Gene, called saying, "Ken, come over tonight. I've figured it out." Charles and Ken gathered that night, with much bubbling enthusiasm, at Gene's home.

The three of us being together increased our enthusiasm. This is going to be "really" good. Better than we had expected.

We headed down the hall to Gene's bedroom. Into Gene's bedroom closet. A walk-in closet – small. Three grown men, one little metal container of film, one developing tank.

We closed the door.

We remembered what the druggist had told us.

There was some light coming in at the top corner of the door. We opened the closet door and put Gene's bathrobe across the corner and closed the door. We blocked that light out.

There was some light coming in at the foot of the door. We took some of Gene's shoes and slippers and shoved them against the foot of the door. We blocked that light out.

There was still some light coming in around the keyhole and the doorknob. I took one of Gene's shirts and held it up against the keyhole and doorknob. We blocked out the last remaining ray of light....

So, we could now *watch* Gene show us how to take the film from the little metal container and place it into the developing tank *in absolute pitch darkness.*

It was really dark.

Absolute pitch darkness.

There was silence.

We were embarrassed.

One of us chuckled.

One of us laughed.

We all laughed.

It was really dark.

Well, we were in the closet. We decided Gene might as well get the one roll of film into the developing tank. He could then at least show us how to mix the chemicals.

He got the film out of the little metal container. Then- it was crowded with three grown men in the closet – someone moved, causing Gene to drop the film. Now, three grown men were searching for a stray sliver of film amid the shoes and slippers in absolute pitch darkness.

Gene's good wife, Ann, came to the door and knocked gently, "Everything all right in there? You've been in there an awfully long time."

There were more academic degrees gathered in that closet than you can imagine. Gene brings two degrees, including a master's degree in engineering. Charles brings three degrees. Yours truly brings four degrees, including a Ph. D. to the closet.

Regrettably, Ann told Julie what had happened in the Dark Closet. And, Ann and Julie had great fun sharing the event with many in the congregation. And, for some time, after that night, people would come up to me, and, almost before they could say anything, they would burst out laughing, or they would try and stifle a hearty chuckle.

We did go to the kitchen that night and learn how to pour the chemicals in the developing tank. And, yes, we did create a solid plan for how each of us would move forward with developing our little metal containers of film with our own developing tanks.

We did well. The film was developed on time.

We did have the best three-screen, three slide projector, multimedia with background music presentation of the mission of our congregation there had ever been. Now and then, throughout the presentation, we would hear a muffled chuckle.

I discovered two important learnings that night. I developed them into two formulas:

$$E - P = D\,C$$

Enthusiasm minus Planning equals a Dark Closet.

Enthusiasm without planning ends up in a Dark Closet. There is no peace in a Dark Closet. A Dark Closet may be humorous. It may be tragic. It is still dark. It is finally no place to be. Enthusiasm without planning goes nowhere. There is no sense of satisfaction, no sense of contentment, no sense of peace. Enthusiasm alone ends up in a Dark Closet....or worse.

Yes, likewise, it is true that planning minus enthusiasm equals sitting still, going nowhere. Many thoughtful plans have gone nowhere because of the assumption that the plan would somehow evoked enthusiasm, and it has not. Planning has merit, but, by itself, it does not develop momentum.

$$E + P = S\,F$$

Enthusiasm plus Planning equals a Strong Future.

Enthusiasm plus planning heads forward, has a sense of movement and a sense of direction. Planning without enthusiasm goes nowhere. There is no movement, no momentum. When we are going nowhere, we are restless, fidgety, aimless, without direction. We are not at peace when we are not moving forward.

We are at peace both when we are moving forward and we know where we are heading. We have a spirit of contentment and a sense of satisfaction, a spirit of confidence and a sense of peace. We know we are heading forward and we are heading toward the future God is encouraging us to discover. Now, we are at peace.

Gene, Charles, and Ken were at peace. We had a sense of satisfaction. Our enthusiasm and our planning had finally come together. We had the best three-screen, three slide projector, multimedia with background music presentation of the mission of our congregation we had ever had. We had an amazing stewardship season. People were extraordinarily generous. We were grateful for what we had learned and for what we had achieved.

When we merge enthusiasm and planning, we find peace.

Opal

"Dr. Callahan, if you cannot help us with anything else while you are here,

at least help us with Opal."

It was mid Thursday afternoon, in late July, waiting for my luggage at the baggage claim of the local airport. The chair of the Administrative Board had come along side me and said those quiet words.

As we were walking to the car, the chair of the Pastor Parish Committee said similar words to me, "Dr. Callahan, if you cannot help us with anything else while you are here, at least help us with Opal."

As we were checking me into the hotel, the Pastor shared the same plea, "Dr. Callahan, if you cannot help us with anything else while you are here, at least help us with Opal."

By Sunday afternoon, more than twenty people had shared their concerns that I help them with Opal. In one way or another, a remarkable range of people had said, "Dr. Callahan, if you cannot help us with anything else while you are here, at least help us with Opal."

Opal was the Church Secretary. She had been the Church Secretary for forty-nine years. This was longer than most people could remember. She had started at twenty-three years of age. Forty-nine years had come and gone. She was now seventy-two years old.

As near as I could tell, it was not age. Across the forty-nine years, even in the early years, she would answer the phone with a loud bellow, "HELLO, ANY ONE THERE?" If the caller asked for the Pastor, she would burst into his office and holler, "PASTOR, PHONE FOR YOU." She would interrupt even when he had some-one with him.

Her own office looked like she had saved and saved and saved every piece of paper she had ever seen. There were stacks and stacks, piles and messes. Cabinets and closets, bookshelves, and desks were piled high. It looked like an ancient attic or an archaic storage shed.

Over the years, the bulletin and newsletter were filled with spell-ing and grammar errors. The ushers, in recent times, had gotten a pool up as to how many errors would be in the Sunday Bulletin. They had found an old offering plate. Each usher would put a dol-lar in the plate and a slip of paper with his name and the number of errors he thought would be in the Sunday Bulletin. The usher with the closest number won the pool of the morning.

On a given Friday, some years before, Opal decided to close the church office at noon. There was not much activity anyway. The phone seldom rang. Hardly anyone came by. The mail came in the morning. She could join her friends for the Friday After-noon Bridge Club. She did not consult with anyone. She simply did it.

On Friday, the second day I was there, we had had a planning meeting over lunch. The Pastor and I were coming back to the church early that Friday afternoon. We found the church locked. The Pastor said, "Oh, that's right. I forgot. Opal closes the church on Friday afternoon. Here, I have my key."

Over the current year, Opal had somehow figured out how to offend fourteen families – one family here, another one there, and so on. These fourteen families had left the church and taken with them a total of forty thousand dollars in giving.

I saved the conversation with Opal for Monday morning. I had been doing the interviews in the Church Library. A small adult Sunday school class met around the library table. It was a quiet space. Comfortable. Peaceful.

I went to Opal's office and invited her to join me in the Library. We walked down the hall together. I held the door to the Library for Opal. We went in.

As we were sitting down at the Library table, Opal said to me, almost in a whisper, "Well, Dr. Callahan, what have you decided to do with me?"

"Opal," I said, "I have decided four recommendations for the Staff-Parish Committee. One, look forward to celebrating your near fifty years of service with your retirement effective September 1 of this year."

"Two, look forward to the third Sunday in September, when everyone is back from vacations, being the Sunday we celebrate your near fifty years of service. We plan to invite the whole church and the whole town. It will be a grand Sunday celebration."

"Three, count on your current salary being your pension as long as you live, and I hope you live a long, long time."

Opal quietly said, "Oh, Dr. Callahan, I'm glad you came my way." She paused. I listened.

She went on, "I know it hasn't been quite as good as it used to be. I didn't have a way forward, and I don't plan to depend on my three children."

By Sunday, I had figured it out.

When Opal was twenty-three years old, her husband deserted her and their three young children. They had been living in a remote, rural area, mostly barely getting by. One day, he just up and walked off. No one ever saw him again.

He simply left.

Opal then had moved to the county seat to look for work, desperately, so her three children could go to the town schools. The only job she could find was as the Church Secretary. She thought she would keep the post for a few years and move on to something better. The years came and went. Her children grew up. She was still there. It had become the only thing she knew.

I had figured it out.

Opal was a proud woman. She had raised her three children. Her oldest son was the leading medical doctor in the county. Her second son was the Judge of the county. Her daughter was the leading business person in the county.

Yes, there had been scholarships and loans, and each of her children had worked hard, and her leadership had helped all of this to come to pass, with her small salary as a Church Secretary.

There had been no money for pension or savings. The church had not provided any form of pension across all of those near fifty years.

She continued to work because that was all the income she had. She was too proud to depend on her children. Year by year, she could see no way forward. She continued as best she could.

I also figured out the loud bellows, "HELLO, ANY ONE THERE?"

In remote, rural areas, in an earlier time, on a party line, that is how people answered the phone No one had taken the time to let her hear herself on the other end of the line in current times.

The bursting into the Pastor's office and hollering, "PASTOR, PHONE FOR YOU" was her effort to please the Pastor.

The stacks and stacks, piles and messes in her office were informally organized. She could find what she was looking for amidst the cabinets and closets, bookshelves, and desks. It was better than the shack in which she had lived in a rural, rural, desolate area of the county.

The spelling and grammar errors in the bulletin and newsletter belonged both to her and to the church. She had never gotten herself to the typing and spelling course, and no one in the church had helped her to get there either. Across the years, there was an embarrassed, good-natured silence on the spelling. The silence was not helpful.

Now, Opal is wise as to how churches work. She said to me, "Dr. Callahan, how long can I depend on my current salary as my pension?" She had seen churches relent on their promises before.

I said, "Opal, I met yesterday, Sunday afternoon, with the following five people. (I named them, the key leaders of the church and of the town.) You have their word that your current salary will be your pension as long as you live, and we all hope you will live for many, many years. Moreover, they plan, with the coming year's budget, to increase your pension by twenty five percent."

This footnote is helpful.

I did not share the following with Opal. In the Sunday afternoon gathering of key leaders I had pointed out to the key leaders that they had lost the forty thousand dollars in giving that had been lost to the church because of the fourteen families leaving because of Opal. They had also paid Opal a twelve thousand dollar salary. The total cost was fifty-two thousand dollars.

There was every possibility that another forty to sixty thousand dollars would walk in the coming years, in lost giving due to Opal offending people. Opal was doing the best she could, and things were not getting better. When they saw it that way, they were more than willing to move forward. And, they had genuine regrets that they had not done well by Opal on a pension before now.

Opal was reassured by the fact that the five key leaders had given their word. Her pension was secured. Then, Opal said, "I am content to retire September 1. I do not think I can come on the third Sunday in September. I might cry."

"Opal," I gently said, "You will not be alone. Many people will be crying. It has been a good near fifty years. People want to share their thanks and appreciation with you. You have done well."

"There is a fourth recommendation I am recommending to the Staff-Parish Committee. You are the one person I have discovered who knows what is happening in both the church and the town. Graduations, Birthdays. Anniversaries. Trips. Awards. New children. Illnesses. Deaths. And on and on. You know what is happening in the lives of people.

"Now, as of September 1, there will be no office. The recommendation is that on each Wednesday morning you bring to your successor the news of the week about people so the news will find its way into the bulletin and the newsletter."

Opal, with a smile of contentment on her face, said, "Oh, Dr. Callahan, could I do that?"

"Yes, it is your gift."

Opal said to me, "Dr. Callahan, I so very much thank you. I am at peace."

Opal retired September 1.

The third Sunday in September was a Day of Appreciation for Opal. It was a day more festive and celebrative than any day the town had ever known.

Opal continues to receive her pension, with the promised increase.

Each Wednesday, she brings by the news of families in the church and in the town.

Opal does well. Opal is at peace.

When we live well, when we finish well, we are at peace.

Grandma Ida and Kate

It was in a small town, not quite a city. Bigger than a village, still small. Tree lined streets. Homes painted white. Shutters on the windows. Gardens of flowers near the front porches.

Everyone knows everyone and has for many generations. The families go back to the early settlers of the area. Farmers. Merchants. Train people. School teachers. Craftsmen.

A railroad goes through the town. At night, the whistle of the ten o'clock train finds most people heading to bed. The main street, filled with shops and stores, has been there for as long as people can remember. A small river meanders through the downtown. The river is quiet and peaceful. The children enjoy wading in the shallow bend of the river.

October is a favorite time of year. The leaves of the old trees turn to their fall colors. The county fair gathers the exhibits, foods, animals, rides, and midway games. The traveling circus brings its rides and games. The merry-go-round is the favorite. The tractor pulls and steer wrestling stir the crowds. The rodeo is great fun.

I was there helping a congregation on the Sunday morning of the opening of the Fair. We were having a good time together. The worship service was stirring and inspiring, warm and welcoming. There was a good group of people attending the service. Everyone was looking forward to the fair.

That Sunday, the choir consisted of about twelve to fourteen singers. They were all in their seventies and eighties.

Save one.

On the second row, where altos frequently sit, there was a young girl. Her choir robe did not hide her condition. She sang with a quiet radiance. She looked peaceful.

I learned of her after church.

Some months before, she had told her parents she was pregnant. Her boyfriend had persuaded her, one time. Her parents were horrified. To be pregnant and unmarried was taboo in this small town. To be pregnant, unmarried, and fifteen was worse than worse.

Her parents threw her out.

She stayed, for a time, with a girl friend and her family. Then, that became awkward. Rumors spread. Her girl friend was accused of sleeping around. Not true. The rumors had done their damage. The girl friend's family asked her to move on.

Her aunt took her in . . . . for a time. After several weeks, the family pressure on her aunt caused her aunt to ask her to leave. They wanted no one in the family to have anything to do with Kate.

For a few nights, Kate had been sleeping in a small shed at the back of the lumberyard. The nights were getting cold. Cooler weather was on the way. Winter would be close behind. She did not know where to turn.

Word had spread. No one would have anything to do with her.

On Sunday morning, she found her way to a church. Not her own church, in which she had grown up. In that last bitter, angry, fiery, eruptive conversation with her parents, she had been warned to never come to the "family" church.

She was cut off.

Kate was drawn to church. She stumbled into this church, not knowing anything about it. She had never been there before. She just could not go on any more.

This congregation was more conservative than her childhood church. Their theology was sterner. Their moral standards were higher. They were of "old stock." They lived mostly in a time that had come and gone. They were of the "old school."

They took her in.

As I write these four words, I marvel at the miracle of that morning.

What moved Grandma Ida to do so, even later, she could not say. As Kate came in the door, and hesitated timidly, Grandma Ida got up from her choir pew and, with a gentle hitch in her step, walked down the aisle to the door, put her arms around Kate, and said, "Welcome home, Kate."

Everyone in the congregation had known of Kate's plight. It was a small town. Many in the congregation knew her girl friend's family, her aunt, her parents, and her whole family. The normal thing would have been to ask her to leave or, perhaps worse, to ignore her . . . . pretend she was not even there.

Grandma Ida would normally have chosen to politely ignore her through the service, and pay no attention to her in the fellowship conversation time following. She could not put into words why she welcomed Kate.

She did say that she was certain Kate was helping her as much as she was helping Kate. Sometimes, the person we are helping is helping us to live our lives at our best.

That Sunday, Kate found her new family.

Grandma Ida took Kate to live with her. Kate became her daughter and the daughter of the whole congregation. In the weeks come and gone, as Kate neared her time, the spirit of compassion and the sense of community deepened in the congregation.

Grandma Ida describes it as "a time of grace and peace." The congregation describes it as a time of expectancy and peace. A child is born. The new family forgives. The grace and peace of God happen.

Grace brings forgiveness. Forgiveness brings peace.

Bitterness and resentment do not bring peace. Anger and animosity do not. Aggression and antagonism do not. Hatred and hostility do not. Grudge and guilt do not. Temper and fury do not.

The grace of forgiveness overcomes all of these. We are at peace.

When we are in *an unforgiving state*, there is no peace. We are out of sorts. We are at loose ends. We are at odds inside and with one another. We are not ourselves.

Forgiveness is peace. With forgiveness, we become ourselves. We become who we really are. We become at peace.

Peace and Forgiveness are good friends.

When we find peace, we find forgiveness.

When we find forgiveness, we find peace.

Mom, Mimi, Aunt Bea

It is interesting how life works.

We had planned the day as a relaxing, fun outing with our extended family and our two young children. The next day, Julie and I were headed overseas, on a research tour of Greece, Egypt, Lebanon, Israel, Palestine, and Turkey.

This day of sailing would be a fun outing together with our larger family. My mom, grandmother, and great aunt would look after our two young sons while we were gone on the journey. Mom was in her early fifties. My grandmother and my Great Aunt Bea were in their seventies.

In the years come and gone since the war, much had happened. The blended family had separated. We had all grown up. Mom, Dad, my grandmother Mimi, and my great Aunt Bea had moved to Florida. The cold and snow of northern Ohio had been too much for them. Florida was better.

Dad was having to work the day we went sailing.

For everyone else, this was a special outing. We were celebrating our family together. We had not had a gathering like this in some time. It was a special time for our two young sons, Ken and Mike, with their grandmother, their great grandmother, their great great aunt, and their mom and dad.

We were having fun.

We had been sailing off the coast of Florida for several hours, heading southeast. It was enjoyable and peaceful. In the morning, the sky was blue, the winds were cool, and the waves were fine. We were having fun, laughing and carrying on, enjoying this special gathering of family.

Sandwiches, chips, and cookies – washed down with lemonade – were enjoyed as we sailed along.

As I look back, I realize that there were four generations of family gathered on the sail boat that day.

As the early afternoon came upon us, we continued to look to the southeast. We could see the storm coming from far off. Julie and I prefer fair-weather sailing, particularly with the passengers we had on board.

The winds were becoming gusty. The waves had more of a chop. The thirty-six-foot sailboat we had rented for a day's sail was due back at 5:00 PM. The clouds in the southeast were becoming darker, more ominous. Massive streaks of lighting began to fill the sky.

Julie and I began to share our concern over the potentially threatening weather. We were sailing toward the southeast, directly toward the storm. Julie and I agreed that a change of course would put us in a better position to return to the harbor entrance when we wanted to go back. We would be closer to the harbor and could more easily reach our dock, particularly if the storm picked up speed in its approach.

Julie and I remarked about these weather signs in a conversational tone with one another. We gently suggested to Mom, Mimi, Aunt Bea, Mike, and Ken that they move to the cabin while we tended to the sails and the changing of course.

We did not call attention to the impending storm. Julie and I stayed calm. We continued to have fun. We shared our suggestion in a calm manner that gave no alarm, with a spirit of peace. Alarm breeds alarm. We did not breed alarm. We stayed calm.

The family continued to enjoy one another's company in the cabin below. They were glad to move below so as not to be in the way as we prepared to deal with the sails and change course. They were having so much fun that they were oblivious to the problems we began to encounter with the boat and the advancing weather.

Julie and I positioned the sails to come about. We were ready.

I moved the tiller to turn the boat.

Nothing happened.

I brought the tiller back to the center position.

I moved the tiller again to turn the boat.

Nothing happened again.

I tried again, moving the tiller, very slowly and deliberately.

Again, nothing happened.

We were still sailing toward the advancing storm.

Leaning over the stern of the boat, I could see that the tiller had separated from the rudder. We still had both the tiller and the rudder; however, they were no longer connected to each other. I could see no way to re-connect them. The necessary connection that does so was now missing.

There was no direct way of "steering" the boat.

And, we were still sailing in the direction of the advancing storm.

I found a long, sturdy line and a bucket. I tied the two together.

We lowered the sails. We needed to negate the effects of the rising winds on the sails of the boat. We did not need the sails to be flapping about as we tried to turn the boat.

We started the inboard motor. The motor would propel the boat. The motor was stationary. It could not turn the boat, but it would give us forward motion.

I lowered the bucket over the starboard side of the boat and slowly played out the long line. The drag of the water in the bucket slowly turned the boat to the north, away from the approaching storm. We had been heading to the southeast, directly toward the storm.

Our harbor was up the coast, several miles to the north and away from the advancing storm. The inboard motor gave us some power. The long line and bucket gave us the ability to steer. We would move the line and bucket to the port side of the boat; then, after a time, we would shift it back to the starboard side of the boat.

Slowly, in a back and forth, catawampus fashion, we worked our way up the coast.

We had been doing this procedure for some time, with good success.

The family down in the cabin was unaware of any danger, enjoying their time together.

Then, I made the mistake of over tacking; the result being that the line got caught in the propeller and the motor stopped. Now, we had no power. The storm was building, coming closer.

I went over the stern, into the water. With some effort, I was able to untangle the line from the propeller. Fortunately, the propeller had not cut the line. The line had stalled the motor before the propeller could damage the line.

Julie and I cleared the line from the propeller. We restarted the motor. We again launched the line and the bucket. We continued our slow, back and forth, catawampus journey up the coast.

As we got near the inlet into the harbor, we encountered more and more boats, both sail and motor. Everyone was returning to beat the storm to their docks.

We needed a tow.

With the long line and the bucket, we were not going to be able to steer into the inlet, with all the other boats, and make the several turns necessary to get to our dock.

We waved.

People waved back.

They thought we were being friendly. They had had a pleasant day out on the ocean as well. It had been great fun.

The waves had become choppier and higher. The lighting strikes were larger and more frequent. The dark clouds seemed thicker. It had begun to rain. The storm was getting closer.

Desperate straits encourage desperate measures.

I asked Julie if she had her half slip on. She did. I suggested she take it off and wave it above her head as an emergency sign. She did.

Immediately, a motor boat came to us. He saw the problem. He threw us a long line. I caught it and tied it down to the bow. With skillful, deft maneuvers, he towed us into the inlet and through the busy harbor to our dock. The full brunt of the storm hit just as we arrived at our dock.

We thanked the men in the other boat. We so were grateful. We were so glad to be safely tied to the secure dock again.

Later, we learned that the part that held the tiller and the rudder together had rusted through, and it had finally given way while we were out sailing that day.

Julie and I had been able to stay calm and to be at peace.

We had worked together as a team. We had exchanged our observations of concern with a gentle spirit. Our voices had stayed quiet and relaxed.

We had shared mutual directions for solving the obstacles we encountered. We got the sails down, started the inboard motor, deployed the long line and the bucket, changed course away from the storm, unwrapped the line from around the propeller, received the tow line from the helping boat, and made our way to our dock.

We were able to do so without raising our voices or getting into fear or anxiety. There was no shouting or yelling. Our situation was too grave to waste energy on excess behaviors like that.

Julie and I were able to work our way through the series of predicaments with reasonable peace and calm – to the extent that when we finally reached the dock, we were all at peace. We had had an enjoyable and fun time.

My mom, grandmother, and great aunt, and our two young sons were having so much fun together that Julie and I decided not to distract them from their fun by calling attention to the impending storm. It was a memorable day of fun for four generations, one of those enchanting days to remember forever.

Julie and I did not make them aware of the advancing storm and the potential danger to us. As long as Julie and I could handle the predicaments as they came up, we would let them continue to have their good fun together.

Julie and I were confident - at peace, as we handled each matter that came up. As a result, the whole group was at peace.

They had enjoyed one another in the cabin below. They had talked and laughed, played games and enjoyed one another's company. They were able to relax and have fun knowing that Julie and I were taking care of sailing the boat, and knowing that we were at peace.

Julie and I worked together as a team, with quiet determination, doing this step, and then this step, and then this step, and then this step to work our way out of our predicament. We did so with a spirit of peace and calm.

One of the arts of living is to express our worries constructively and helpfully. We can share how we actually feel about something without, at the same time, doing so in a way that is harmful to those we love, without shouting or commotion, scolding and complaining, whining and lamenting.

Sometimes, we allow our feelings to get the best of us. Sometimes, we keep our feelings inside. We bottle them up. We repress them. We clam up.

Then some trigger event happens. We overreact

The pendulum swings wildly, rushingly to the other extreme. Before we know it, we are shouting, crying, intensely, bitterly, and hurtfully saying things that leap from our mouths; even as we try to trap the words before they escape, they rush forth, bringing even more words behind them.

There are too many words we wish had never escaped from our mouths. We are ashamed. There are too many deeds we wish we had never done. We are embarrassed. Then, we have to figure out how to make amends, to apologize, to right the wrongs that the words have caused, that *we* have caused.

Sometimes, we have learned a negative, hurtful way of sharing our fears and anxieties. There is nothing positive about that way. If we have figured out how to learn that negative way, then we can figure out a more helpful way. If we have learned a destructive habit, we can learn a constructive habit. With honor and integrity, we can share our worries with peace and calm.

We can share constructive feelings of praise and thankfulness, appreciation and compassion: "Well done!" When we are anxious, we can share our anxiety without blaming those around us: "I'm concerned about the dark clouds ahead."

When we are fearful, we can share our fears – without frightening those we love. "The lighting is more frequent." We can say this in a calm, peaceful way. When we are anxious, we can share our anxieties simply and straightforwardly, without being hard on those we love and causing them more anxiety.

We can learn to share our peace.

We are created with a sense of peace about living. When we learn how to express our sense of peace, we encourage others to be at peace.

Alarm breeds alarm. Fear breeds fear. Peace breeds peace. We can learn how to express our feelings with peace and calm. We can learn how to express our joy, our fun, and our good times.

As we learn how to express these positive feelings, we also learn how to express our feelings of anxiety, fear, anger, resentment, guilt, and bitterness constructively. As we discover peaceful ways to share joy and compassion, laughter and good fun, we can also learn the capacity to make amends. Likewise, as we learn how to share our feelings of fear and anger constructively, we discover richer, fuller ways to share our sense of joy and peace in living.

Jesus describes the Kingdom of God as a wedding feast, as a great banquet. This life is a wedding feast of joy and wonder, a great banquet of grace and peace. As we experience the grace and peace of God, we learn the capacity to share grace and peace with those around us.

My mom, grandmother, great aunt, and our two young sons gave Julie and me the encouragement to work through our series of severe predicaments with grace and peace. In tough times, be at peace. You will handle the tough times better.

Tough times are tough enough by themselves. When we add anxiety and fear, anger and rage, shouting and uproar, upsetness and confusion, we make the tough times even tougher.

When times are tough, be at peace.

St. John's

It was in the spring. There had been much snow during the winter. Good rains had come in the early spring. The trees, grasses, and flowers were in full bloom. The peace and beauty of the landscape was rich and lush. It was an amazing time of year.

I was helping one congregation.

We were gathered in the sanctuary, praying and puzzling for the future of their congregation. One of the best things we do as Christians is pray. They had had thirty-seven losing seasons. They had had nearly four decades of slowly declining and dying. We needed to gather all the prayers we could.

Mostly, these were good-natured, well-intentioned people. They had become preoccupied with their decline. They thought of themselves as a losing team. They had closed in upon themselves. They had allowed themselves to stay in their Dark Closet.

And, with each successful losing season, they had further convinced themselves, even more so, that they were a losing congregation. They could see no way forward.

They had tried this and that. With good intentions, they had tried every gimmick and gadget, trick and triviality, data and demographic, chart and graph, program and pleasantry that had come down the track. For the moment, there would be a quick flourish of excitement; then, slowly, steadily, a withering of interest and further decline.

They could not seem to draw people into their church.

Their focus had been on how to get people inside their church. After all, they were getting older. There were more funerals each year. The church was dying off. More pews were empty. Fewer givers were giving. It was becoming harder and harder to afford to keep the doors open, the lights on, and the grass mowed.

A whispered anxious spirit had settled, like a gray mist, an ancient shroud, over the congregation. Mary was gone. Harold was gone. Wilbur's pew was empty. Sue no longer sang in the choir. Walter was not there as an usher. The names went on and on....of who was missing. We were nervous and anxious. We were unsettled.

There was no peace.

As we were praying that day, I noted that in the center of the chancel, the main aisle leads up to it, the altar stands in front of it, they have a remarkable stained glass window of Christ standing at the door, knocking.

You remember the picture, the window, the Biblical image.

In the long, lost churched culture of an earlier time, the understanding of the picture, the window, the Biblical image was, "Christ stands at the door, knocking, hoping someone will hear the knock, and come to the door, and open the door, and invite Christ **in** to their lives."

Much was made of the fact that there was no doorknob or latchstring or keyhole on the outside of the door. We would be the ones who would hear the knock and we would be the ones to come to the door and we would be the ones to open the door and we would be the ones to invite Christ **in** to our lives.

It dawned on me that day as we were kneeling at the altar rail, praying, with the sunlight streaming through the stained glass window in a remarkable way, what the picture, the window, the Biblical image means in our time:

"Christ stands at the door, knocking,
hoping someone will hear the knock,
and come to the door, and open the door
so Christ can invite them **out** to his life, serving in the world.

Good friends, it is no longer that we invite Christ **in** to our lives.
Now, Christ invites us **out to his life.**
Where is Christ?
Serving the world. Serving the mission.
Where does Christ live and die and is risen again and again?
Among the human hurts and hopes God has planted all around us.

Christ is in the world. When we are in the world, we are with Christ. It is not that we discover Christ, then go and serve in mission. It is in the sharing of the mission that we discover Christ.

In this new day, Christ invites us **out** . . . . to live and serve with him in the world....in mission.

Our focus had been on how to get people **in** our church. Christ's focus has been on how to get us **out**, serving in God's world.

When we discover Christ's invitation to be with him – out, serving the world, we are at peace. We are calm. We know we have found what really counts in this life. Anxiety and worry leave us. Peace and contentment join us.

We discussed this, the people of St. John's and myself. For years on end, the goal had been how to get people **in** the church. Now, the goal could be how to get the congregation **out**, serving the world.

A gentle calm came over the congregation. A spirit of contentment settled over the congregation. A quiet peace descended over the people.

There would be no further worry or hustle over whether we could get people to come in to the church, to fill the pews. It had not worked very well anyway. And, we had been too nervous and anxious. No one is drawn to a group that is nervous and anxious.

People are nervous and anxious enough. They do not need the mixed blessing of a group that makes them more nervous and anxious. They are looking for a grouping that is living in grace and peace.

St. John's discovered a mission with children and a mission with grandparents. The children thrive. The grand parents thrive. St. John's is at peace.

When we serve, we thrive. We find grace and peace. We gain confidence and assurance. We discover our strengths. We serve well. When we strive, we do not thrive. It is counter-productive. We become nervous and anxious.

Be at peace. We give ourselves away with Christ, serving the world. We answer Christ's invitation to be with him, out among the people God has planted all around us. We are no longer worried about filling our pews. We focus on filling people's lives with grace and peace.

When we focus on giving grace and peace, we find grace and peace.

When we find the world, we find peace.

$\mathcal{D}orothy$

Dorothy would call early.

There was a whole series of Saturday mornings when she would call and say something like, "Ken, I'm in the bathroom. The razor blades are on the counter. I can't take it any more. I'm just calling to say good-bye."

Her phone call really was an urgent invitation to talk her through till sunrise. Or, while Julie held the fort on the phone, I would rush over to help.

Dorothy was not crying "wolf." These were not "wolf, wolf, wolf" phone calls. They were dead serious. She knew how to slash her wrists the correct way to make it to "the other side of the river." And, in an earlier time, she had nearly succeeded three times.

I finally figured out her fear: it was chaos.

In her early growing up years, she had met chaos full blown. Her two parents were full-blown, blooming, top-of-the-line, raging alcoholics. They fought all the time. Drinking and fighting were their favorite pastimes. The house was always a mess, a junk heap, stuff piled on stuff. Pandemonium reigned. The house was always in chaos. Life was always chaos.

Dorothy never invited any friends over. The mess was too much. The on-going fights of her parents were too strident and raucous, noisy and loud. And yet, at the same time, in search of some peace,

47

Dorothy's room was immaculate. Everything was in order. Everything had its proper place. It was always in its place. Her room was the quiet haven against bedlam and chaos. It was her haven of peace.

In time, she grew up and moved away. Some of the patterns of her parents went with her. Wherever she lived was always neat and clean. However, she had fallen into the pattern of becoming an alcoholic herself. She had learned from two pros, her parents. She did it well.

She went through quite a patch of difficulty. She had several years of hard drinking. Her alcoholism was getting the best of her. She found an AA group. She did her 12 Steps. She had stayed sober for a long, long time. She had some difficulty. She stayed sober. She still had trouble with her early demon....chaos.

In her work, she was praised for her exacting, precise, superior work. She moved ahead from one promotion to the next. With each promotion came more pressure, more confusion, and more chaos.

Her weekends became more and more chaotic....

Dorothy was fearful of chaos....

Dorothy's work, her job, delivered her sufficient structure that she could make it through the week. Friday at five o'clock she entered a world of chaos, a world of no structure. By early Saturday morning, with her fears, her anxieties, her terror of chaos, she was ready to call this world quits.

I began a proactive approach – I would call Dorothy at work, on Friday morning, at her ten o'clock break. She had a sheet of paper and a pencil. I had a sheet of paper and a pencil. Together, we would structure her weekend.

Who she would see. Where she would go. What she would do. We put together a detailed schedule, based on thirty minute increments, which organized her time from five o'clock Friday afternoon to early Saturday morning. It was like her work schedule. Then, we organized her schedule, in detail, for both Saturday and Sunday.

It worked....the first week.

It worked....the second week.

Then, it didn't work.

It did.

It didn't. It didn't. It didn't.

It did. It did. It did.

It didn't.

Then, it did, and did and did and did....

Dorothy, Julie, and I celebrated.

Several years went by. Dorothy called.

She had been transferred some years before to another city. She had flourished in her work and in her life. She was coming through town and hoped we could visit over lunch. Certainly. We would look forward to being together.

We gathered at one of our favorite restaurants. Dorothy, Julie, and myself. We were delighted and excited to be together. It had been some time.

Our server came. We ordered. The special that day looked very good.

Dorothy brought us up-to-date on all that was happening in her life. We shared with her about the doings and developments in our lives. It was a grand reunion of old friends who had been through much together.

Over dessert, Dorothy shared with us why she wanted to have lunch.

She wanted to thank us for all those times on those early Saturday mornings, I had talked her through till sunrise, or while Julie held the fort on the phone, I would rush over to help. She wanted to thank us for helping her to be alive.

Most especially, she wanted to thank me for the ten minute phone calls on those Friday mornings at her ten o'clock break.

She said to us, "I want you to know that it was in those Friday morning phone calls that I began to learn how to take control of my life. I learned how to lead my own life."

As Dorothy shared these words, each of us experienced the spirit of being at peace. We were at peace. Life is good. God blesses us with grace and peace.

With Dorothy, I learned these two wonderful insights,

Share almost enough help to be helpful.

Do not share so much help that the help becomes harmful and creates a pattern of dependant and co-dependent behavior.

The ten-minute phone calls on the Friday mornings were more helpful than the phone calls talking Dorothy through to sunrise or the many rushing overs in the early mornings.

Peace comes with delivering almost enough help to be helpful. We share experience and wisdom, coaching and encouraging. Almost enough. Not too much. We do not over-coach or over-help. We are at peace.

When some urgency comes to us, some emergency, and we give too much help, we will not be at peace. We will have taken the emergency on ourselves. We will have taken the emergency away from the person. When we do that, the person cannot do anything about their own dilemma. We have taken it away. We will have made the dilemma our dilemma. We will have no peace.

My wisdom teaches me that we sometimes do this because we want to be too helpful. We may have not helped in some situations. Not helping in some situations may cause us, out of guilt, to help too much in others. We experience a sense of guilt. We over help in other situations to assuage our guilt.

Or, it could be that we have developed a pattern, a habit, a routine of simply over- helping. For whatever reasons, we offer too much help - more help than helps. It is almost automatic. We plunge in. We do everything we can....and then some.

Or, it could be that we confuse forgiving and helping. We are encouraged to forgive seventy times seven. Our forgiving this much is difficult. What we are encouraged to forgive is grievous and appalling. We are uncertain we can forgive with this generosity.

We sometimes imagine that we can compensate for our difficulties in forgiving by over-helping. But, over-helping does not help with forgiving. Over-helping only confuses us with our capacity for forgiving. Focus on forgiving for its own integrity, for its own healing value.

Helping is a separate matter.

Sometimes, we offer no help. The urgency, the emergency does not resonate with us. We are tired. We are busy. It does not quite fit. We are overwhelmed. We decide to pass. We decide to not help. Strange to say, this, in some situations, is the best way to help.

Now, not helping is not an excuse for not helping. With wisdom and compassion, we assess whether we are in the best position to be of help.

It may well be that our strengths, gifts, and competencies do not match with the emergency. Our best help, then, is to refer the person to an individual or grouping whose gifts and competencies match with the situation.

My wisdom teaches me that the helpful "first choice" is this: when your strengths match with the urgency, offer *almost* enough help. This is the art of helping. You will be at peace. The problem will stay with the person. Both of you will move forward.

Next best is to offer no help. With compassion and wisdom, you recognize that your strengths, gifts, and competencies do not mach with the dilemma at hand. You can refer the person to an individual or a group who can be of help. You will have helped. You will be at peace.

The "least helpful choice" is to offer too much help. That is.... *to over-help.* To offer too much help has no merit. It does more damage and harm than help. There is, finally, no help. There is no peace.

With the first choice, you will be at peace. With the second choice, you will be at peace. With the third choice, you will not be at peace.

Learn from Dorothy.

Share just enough help, and be at peace.

Grand Children

Peace has more to do with people than with parking.

A good friend of mine shared this event with me. He calls the event, "Who's that parking in my space?"

It was Sunday morning. He and his wife have always had a steady, balanced schedule for getting ready for church. Their routine assures them that they are always on time. He said that for some reason, that morning they were running ten minutes late.

I could not find my shoes. They were not in the bedroom where I thought they had been the night before. I found them in the breakfast room.

I finally found the car keys. They were on the kitchen counter.

Then, I found my glasses. On the night stand.

We were walking out the door.

Late.

The phone rang. It was Aunt Wilda. She had some question about where everyone was gathering for Sunday dinner after church. We talked briefly.

Then, we were on our way. Fifteen minutes late.

Late.

I made up five minutes. We were still ten minutes late. In years upon years of going to my church, I had never....never been late before.

I pulled into the parking lot and made my usual right turn toward my regular parking space.

I have parked in that same place for years upon years.

I have sat in the same pew for the same number of years.

I have filed deeds on both at the nearby county courthouse.

Everyone knows where I park and where I sit. Most other leaders have their own parking space and pew as well.

Someone was pulling into my parking space.

A new blue SUV.

Who's that parking in my space? *I said this to myself. Then, I said it out loud to my wife.*

Then, I added, who has the nerve to park in my space?

I was frustrated. We were late, and never had been.

I like things to be in their place.

This morning everything seemed to have come unglued.

I was getting even more upset.

I almost honked my horn.

Just as I began to press down on the horn, I saw my son get out of the new blue SUV car. I had forgotten. My son and his wife had just bought a new car. They were very pleased with it. There was more room for their children.

*My first impulse was to ask him to move **his** car from **my** space.*

Then, I remembered he had ridden with his mother and me to church, as a young child and as a youth, as a passenger in our family car. He was familiar with that same space. It was the space he had always "parked" in.

His memories of coming to church must have led him to this space.

Fortunately, I was slow to say anything.

Years later, I am still grateful I had been slow to say anything.

This was the first time they had been to church in years.

My son and his wife had been married some seven years before. It was a lovely wedding. They were a wonderful couple. They belonged together. They had found each other in college. They had dated for three years. After graduation, they had married.

Shortly after their wedding, his company had transferred him to another city. He did well. The firm was pleased with his work. They began to have children. With the transfer and the coming of children, they had not found, for whatever reasons, another church.

We had visited them often. We enjoyed our family times together. As the children were born, we were glad to go and help. They were emerging as a wonderful family. Each new child was, for us, a new grand child. We were delighted.

As the saying goes, "If we had known how much fun grandchildren were going to be, we would have had them first."

The oldest, Timmy, was seven. He was quiet and studious, bent on achieving and accomplishing. The middle child, Billy, was five. He was earnest about sports, especially baseball. The youngest, Johnny, was three. He was very social. He meets many new friends. He loves people. All three are a joy.

A couple of months before the Sunday of his parking in my parking space, the company had transferred them back to our city. We were overjoyed to have them now home again. We enjoyed getting together with them, for cookouts and outings at the lake. We would go over to their new home. They would come over to our home. We were having wonderful times together.

They had come to church that morning to surprise us. He had just naturally gone to the parking space he knew.

Our three grandchildren climbed out of the back seats of their new blue SUV. They saw me. They smiled and laughed. They radiated happiness. "Grandpa, we are coming to church with you today." They ran to our car, smiling and laughing.

I got out. I hugged each one. They bubbled with joy and love. They ran around to the other side of the car to hug their grandmother. They were so excited. "We are going to church with you, today," they sang with joy, bouncing up and down.

I said to my son, "It is great to see you. Your mother and I will be right in. We're happy we can worship together this morning. It is wonderful you are home."

My wife and I parked in a distant space, at the back of the lot. It was the next-to-the last empty space in the lot.

As we walked to the church, I said to her, "Phyllis, this a wonderful Sunday. Our family is finally fully together now. Let's celebrate and be generous. Let's help the church buy the vacant lot next door.

"It has been for sale for a long time. I know the owner. We can do it. We talked about this idea earlier. Look. This is a normal Sunday. The parking is full. We can plan on helping our grandchildren worship with us. We'll help buy the vacant lot and give it to the church."

And they did.

There was a spirit of peace about him that Sunday.

There was a spirit of peace about him as he shared the story with me.

A generous spirit brings peace.

When we live with a generous spirit, we are at peace.

Orville

Orville loved children. That is the simplest, easiest way to describe the life and mission of this remarkable man. He was the principal of the Brady Lake Elementary School and, for years upon years, he was the most beloved person in the community.

He had a hearty laugh, a generous spirit, and wonderful wisdom. He had a marvelous capacity to discern the gentlest ways to encourage children. His encouraging grace freed kids to discover their strengths. He was beloved by the children, the parents, the grandparents, and the teachers.

He was not tall. He was stocky, balding, with most of his hair gone. He was on his way to having the build of a wonderful Santa Claus. He walked with kind of a skip, as though he was having fun. He had a wonderful spirit of humility, grace, and peace.

He recruited the best teachers for his elementary school. He encouraged them well. He did the best to help them advance their training. He secured generous supplies for their classes. He knew the children by name. He had had most of their parents in school when they were younger.

He and Mary lived on a small peninsula on Brady Lake. They enjoyed the changing seasons of the year. They took pleasure in having friends and family over often. Orville loved to cook barbeque.

He had had fun entertaining the people of the community. Their home was a gathering place for the community.

He was a legend.

The offers came year after year. "We have a bigger school for you." "We have a better school for you." "We have a newer school for you." "You would be the ideal principal for the new high school." "There is the promotion to the County Education Office." "We would love for you to move to our county in another part of the state and be our superintendent of schools."

Orville stayed.

Brady Lake was a small community of plain, older homes, mostly small, not fancy, gathered around a modest, clear blue lake. People enjoyed reasonable fishing in the summer, the wonderful turning of the trees in autumn, ice-skating in the winter, the fields coming to new life in the spring.

Farms nestled up to the homes. These were old farms, with great barns built on enormous barnstone foundations. The crops came from apple orchards, cornfields, and strawberry patches. Some farms had a few cows. These were unassuming farms, not wealthy farms. They were cared for by plain, decent people.

One of the farms had a grand old cider mill. People would come from miles around for the freshly made cider, the newly picked apples, the pies, the candies, and the gathering of families.

Orville was content.

He knew he had found his mission: the children of Brady Lake. He knew he was in the right place with the right group. He felt led to help these children. He could relate to these kids. He knew what growing up was like in this community.

He had discovered his longings and his competencies. He shared concrete, effective help. He lived a life of unconditional service. His help was freely given. Countless lives were helped by this one wise, caring man who went about his quiet and unassuming mission year in and year out.

He was at peace with his life because he was at peace with his mission. Peace is often found in mission. God invites us to a life of serving, not a life of surviving, nor a life of striving. We are not invited to a life that is self-centered and self-seeking.

Amidst the competing attractions of this life, the fleeting flimsies that tempt us, the transitory captivations that abound, we are whole and healthy when we discover a life of mission and peace.

God plants within each human heart longings to help. These longings frequently focus on a specific human hurt and hope. Wherever there is a hurt, there is a hope. Some people see their mission in helping a particular person who means much to them.

Many see their mission in helping their children and grandchildren develop into constructive adults. For some, a community interest – such as education, safety, housing, or poverty – stirs their longings to help.

We want our lives to *count*.

Not necessarily in any grandiose way, but in some enduring way. We want to know that, having lived our lives, our life has had some value, has not been lived for nothing. Some people have benefited. The art of life is to discover one's mission. The joy of life is to serve well.

Our lives can be counting in some enduring way. When we are serving others, we are participating in the mission of God. The question of the culture, "What do you do?" has usually been answered with a description of our job. The deeper search in our lives, sometimes not consciously realized, is the question of mission.

Who is our mission? For Orville, it was the children of Brady Lake.

God gives us these gifts: our longings to help, our matching strengths and competencies, our ability to freely give, and our capacity to share our help. We grow as we serve. We live as we share.

Peace and Mission are good friends. When we discover our mission, we discover peace. We are restless without our sense of mission. We long and yearn for our lives to count in some spirit of mission. Mission is the breath of life, the peace of life. We are at peace. We live in peace.

When we live our mission, we are at peace.

Julie and Ken

Peace may be found beyond the end of forever.

Julie and I were on a trip together. We were in a major city of a restful, enchanting country. Two wonderful, large islands are the country. The people are gracious. The hillsides are green. Open spaces abound. We were having great fun.

We enjoy peaceful, unstructured, adventurous exploring.

We secured a hire car. We headed out to see the remote regions of the north island. We got the best map we could find. We decided to head north, to the outer reaches of the island, to see where the land meets the ocean.

I noticed on the map that the modest paved road in the city quickly gave way, just beyond the city, to a little dirt road. I traced the road on the map. The dirt road continued for a while, getting narrower; then, on the map, the word "unknown" was written.

Several times.

The map maker wanted people to know they would now be in the unknown.

On the map, the dirt road on which we planned to travel seemed to end at what looked like a tree. By the drawing of the tree, there were two words: "Black Stump". I asked the person who sold us the map what that meant.

She said, "The black stump is our way of saying that past this point is beyond the end of forever."

I noted to her that, on the map, the distance from the Black Stump to the edge of the ocean looked to be a considerable number of miles. I asked, "Is there a road from the Black Stump on to the ocean?" With a twinkle in her eyes, she said, "You be surprised. Enjoy your trip."

Julie and I headed out.

Time and miles passed.

We passed through a wonderful countryside with rolling hills and ancient trees. We saw an occasional cottage. Not large. Modest. With flowers planted around it. The farther we went the fewer the homes we saw. There were now miles upon miles of open, spacious land, tall gangly trees, and meandering, small streams.

We came to the Black Stump.

We were a bit taken aback. It actually was the Black Stump.

It was off to the side of the road, a huge old tree stump, black, withered, worn, still strong. A sign proclaimed its purpose. Flowers grew around it. The dirt road on which we had been traveling continued, much to our delight and surprise. It was very narrow and quite bumpy.

We said, "Well, the road is not on the map, but here it is. Let's give it a go."

We found ourselves traveling in some of the most beautiful parts of that country. The trees seemed taller and greener. The grass was richer and thicker. We saw more birds and wildlife. No people. It was serene and enchanting.

No one seemed to live there. We continued on.

After a long time, the road made a slow, gentle turn to the left, and as we came around the bend, we saw an ancient, stately lighthouse, with a small, whitewashed, now empty cottage beside it.

We pulled our hire car to a stop and got out.

A peaceful quiet surrounded us. Birds lifted their voices in song. Then, they were quiet. Then, they sang again. It was magic.

We walked around the ancient lighthouse and stood at the edge of the cliff. There, we looked out on the most amazing sight.

Two separate seas came together and joined as one just off that coast. One had a rich, coral color, the other a brighter, deeper blue. The sun shone brightly, dancing across the gently rolling waves.

It was as if we had discovered a completely new world.

A world of coral and a world of blue coming together as one. A world of peace and contentment filling our hearts with the mystery of God's amazing creation. We were silent with awe. We were at peace.

I can see it now.

The sea and the ocean sharing the peace and grace of life. We were seeing beyond the end of forever. We were at peace.

On January 1, 1925, Edwin Hubble, in his paper, helped the world to discover that the universe is more than the Milky Way. Since then, not yet one hundred years, with our modern telescopes and space explorations, we have discovered that the universe seems to extend forever. Space and time extend beyond the end of forever.

God creates the universe as immense as it is so we will know how immense the grace and peace of God is for us. God creates seas of coral and oceans of blue so we will discover beyond the end of forever.

God's steadfast grace and peace endure forever . . . even beyond the end of forever. God gives us this New World. The grace of God surrounds us. The compassion of Christ sustains us. The peace and hope of the Holy Spirit leads us.

We live whole, healthy lives. God blesses us with the seas of coral and the oceans of blue. God invites us to new possibilities. God gives us grace, peace, and hope.

Be at peace.

The peace of God extends even beyond the end of forever.

Endings

PRACTICE PEACE

You are welcome to practice the art of being at peace.

When we practice peace, we do so with an easy, gentle spirit, not too strident. When we try too hard to *make* a life of peace, it has the opposite effect. We become too tense, tight, nervous, and anxious.

When we relax and receive the grace of God, our life overflows with generous moments of peace.

In life, we can count on and depend upon moments of peace now here, now there, like the grace of God. For this moment, we experience the peace of God. And, now, for this moment, we experience the grace of God.

It is quite different from a compulsive addictive perfectionism that creates a fixation that we *will* live a life of peace *all* of the time.

You are welcome to think of the events with which you experience peace the most. Practice being involved in these events. Spend less time with events that do not bring you peace. Some events have a high onset of frustration and confusion. Spend less time with these.

Some persons draw out our lesser selves. Their low self-esteem rubs off on us.

Their fears and anxieties increase ours. Their resentments and bitternesses remind us of ours. Their complainings and lamentings prompt us to become passively critical of ourselves.

In life, there are some days that are dim. Some days are dark. Some days seem desolate and dismal, barren and bleak, gloomy and depressing. God is there with us in just such times. Look for the grace and peace of God.

Whatever events you most enjoy, do these events more frequently. Whatever persons you have the most fun with, spend more time with these persons. Practice peace while being with these persons. Happy persons, who live in grace and peace, will bless you with their grace and peace.

When you are visiting with someone new, someone that you have just met, say to yourself, "Be at peace." You will be. Show a genuine interest in the new person. You can invite them to share about themselves. You will come mutually to know one another. You will develop a new friend.

When you are going on vacation, say to yourself, "Have fun. Be at peace."

Work and worries are behind. Schedules and appointments are only for enjoyment.

Focus on having fun. Be at peace.

When you are golfing, just before you swing the club, breathe in and breathe out, and say to yourself these words,

"Be at peace."

Saying these words in a soft, gentle, affirming way will help you to hit an excellent ball.

If, just before you swing, you say, "Don't hit it too hard," you will. The last word in your mind is "hard." That is what you will do. You will tighten up and, in the last second of your swing, you will hit it too hard. Now, you will have to go and find the ball.

When you are giving a presentation, just before you begin, say to yourself, "Be at peace." You will be. Your presentation will share grace and compassion, wisdom and confidence, peace and assurance.

When you are digging a ditch, say to yourself, "Be at peace." Do not focus on how hard the dirt is, or how hot the weather is. Dig a straight ditch. Deep enough, with enough width to do the job. Be at peace.

When you are doing household chores, say to yourself, "Be at peace," and you will be. The chores will move forward with a spirit of ease and contentment. If you do the chores with a sense of resentment and umbrage, that is what they will be. You can choose. Be at peace.

When you are visiting in the hospital, worried over a loved one, say to yourself, "Be at peace." Pray for the grace and peace of God. Weep. Cry. Visit quietly. Encourage.

Share love and compassion. Trust in God. Be at peace.

When you are planting a garden, as you begin the planting, say to yourself, "Be at peace." As you plant each flower and vegetable, say these words again. "Be at peace."

Bless each flower and vegetable.

As best you can, in day-to-day life, be at peace.

POSSIBILITIES FOR PEACE

I call these *possibilities for peace*. They are more than lessons. The term *lessons* has a fixed, static sense. It is as though a lesson is once learned, and is now a fixed part of one's makeup. A lesson is something that has happened, and, then, we move on. Life is more dynamic than that.

A possibility is something we discover each day, new and fresh. Each day, with newfound wonder and deep, amazing joy, we learn, we discover anew, the possibility that has come to us in some event that has happened in our lives. We discover new possibilities, new persons, new feelings, new meanings, and new ways forward. Peace-filled events continue to change our life and shape our destiny.

This book contains several possibilities for discovering moments of peace.

These events are helpful for developing, thinking, encouraging possibilities for peace. These events have shaped me, and many of the persons, groupings, and communities with whom I have shared.

We have found new discoveries, deeper strengths, and richer possibilities from these events. You are welcome to enjoy these events and discover the learnings that will help you live in the grace of God. Have fun.

Where life abounds, grace abounds. Where grace abounds, life abounds. With these wonderful persons, in these several events, in these superb possibilities, the grace and peace of God abounds.

1. When we find home, we are at peace. Eunice and Mrs. Perkins

2. When we merge enthusiasm and planning, we find peace. Gene, Charles, Ken

3. When we live well, when we finish well, we are at peace. Opal

4. When we find forgiveness, we find peace. Grandma Ida and Kate

5. When times are tough, be at peace.	Mom, Mimi, and Aunt Bea
6. When we find the world, we find peace.	St. John's
7. Share just enough help, and be at peace.	Dorothy
8. When we live with a generous spirit, we are at peace.	Grand Children
9. When we live our mission, we are at peace.	Orville
10. Be at peace. The peace of God extends even beyond the end of forever.	Julie and Ken

These possibilities, these living events, these persons give you ways you can practice peace in your own life.

We long for peace. We yearn for peace.

Peace is not a matter of treaties, truces, and treatises. These have their value. They sometimes help. And, they last for a day, or a season, or a year. Peace is not a matter of coalitions and consortiums, trenches and battlefields. These, too, last for a day, or a season, or a year.

Kingdoms rise and fall. Empires come and go. Societies and cultures stir and disappear. War and wind, fighting and fury clash across the battlements. Fathers and mothers are lost. Sons and daughters are gone. Grandchildren are no more. Generation after generation is given over to the fighting.

Peace is not created, finally, from the "top down" of a culture, nation, or society.

Sometimes, it seems as if peace comes and goes, like the shifting winds of a summer season. Peace is here. Then, it is gone. Now, we enjoy the gentle quiet of peace. Then, it disappears.

Peace, finally, is a grassroots spirit that moves across the land. Peace moves from one person to the next, encouraging one another to live in peace. Peace is gently stirring and contagious.

You can encourage a spirit of peace in yourself. You can be at peace. If only one person around you can be at peace, you can let yourself be at peace. You can live in peace. With the gift of God's peace, you can create a circle of peace in and around yourself.

You can encourage your loved ones and friends to be at peace. They will benefit by living in peace. You will bless them with peace and they will bless you. You can encourage a circle of peace around your loved ones and friends.

You can encourage your neighbors and associates to be at peace. You will encourage them to a spirit of calm and contentment. They will be at peace. You can encourage a circle of peace within and around your neighbors and associates.

These three circles of peace will bless all of the persons within them. Moreover, these three circles will radiate across the world. Peace begins at home. Peace begins with you.

You can receive the peace God gives you.

Living in peace helps us to live whole, healthy lives in the grace of God.

ENJOY PEACE, A GIFT

Peace and Grace are good friends.

Enjoy peace. When you experience a moment of peace, savor this precious moment. When we experience grace, we discover peace. It is not that we have to manufacture peace, try to *make* peace. Peace comes as a gift. The gift of grace is the gift of peace.

When we experience the grace of God, we receive the peace of God. Peace is not something we do. Peace is the generous gift of God.

We are amazed. We do not resent the gift of peace. We are overwhelmed. We do not reject the gift of peace. We are in awe. We are not bitter. We have wonder and joy. We do not become cynical. Yes, we are not worthy of the gift of peace. We are grateful.

In the King James Bible, Cambridge Edition, in John 14:27, we discover these words,

> Peace I leave with you,
> my peace I give unto you:
> not as the world giveth,
> give I unto you.
> Let not your heart be troubled,
> neither let it be afraid.

The world gives peace in the comfort of material things, in honors and pedestals, in prestige and pride, in status and station. The world gives peace in the bits and pieces of stuff, in the fabrics and the objects of this world. These have their time and their comfort.

Lasting peace comes in the grace and peace and hope of God. This deeper peace is the gift of God.

We rejoice. We enjoy the wonder of peace in our lives.

We discover simple, gentle grace.

We hear the quiet words of God, "Be at Peace."

We are at peace.

Peace be with you and bless you,
now
and beyond the end of forever....

Be at Peace....

SELECTED BIBLE RESOURCES

Peace I leave with you, my peace I give unto you:
not as the world giveth, give I unto you.
Let not your heart be troubled, neither let it be afraid.
John 14:27

And the peace of God, which passeth all understanding,
shall keep your hearts and minds through Christ Jesus.
Philippians 4:7

Now the Lord of peace himself
gives you peace always by all means.
2 Thessalonians 3:16

If it be possible, as much as it is in you,
live peaceably with all men.
Romans 12:18

Thou wilt keep him in perfect peace, whose mind is stayed on thee:
because he trusteth in thee.
Isaiah 26:3

Those things, which ye have both learned,
and received, and heard, and seen in me, do:
and the God of peace shall be with you.
Philippians 4:9

For the mountains shall depart, and the hills be removed;
but my kindness shall not depart from thee,
neither shall the covenant of my peace be removed,
saith the LORD that hath mercy on thee.
Isaiah 54:10

Grace to you, and peace,
from God our Father and the Lord Jesus Christ.
Philemon 1:3

Let us therefore follow after the things which make for peace,
and things wherewith one may edify another.
Romans 14:19

Blessed are the peacemakers:
for they shall be called the children of God.
Matthew 5:9

Therefore being justified by faith,
we have peace with God through our Lord Jesus Christ.
Romans 5:1

For ye shall go out with joy, and be led forth with peace:
the mountains and the hills shall break forth
before you into singing,
and all the trees of the field shall clap their hands.
Isaiah 55:12

Glory to God in the highest,
and on earth peace,
good will toward men.
Luke 2:14

Now the God of peace be with you all.
Amen
Romans 15:33

Author

KENNON L. CALLAHAN, PH. D.

Kennon L. Callahan - author, researcher, professor, theologian, and pastor - is a number one bestselling author and among today's most sought-after speakers and consultants.

Dr. Callahan's newest and twentieth book is **Living in Peace**.

He has worked with thousands of groupings around the world and has helped tens of thousands of persons and leaders. His helpful seminars are filled with encouragement, compassion, wisdom, and practical possibilities.

Dr. Callahan's research travels have led him to all of the states in the United States, all of the provinces in Canada, the Arctic, Norway, Holland, England, Denmark, Sweden, Finland, Estonia, Germany, Russia, Turkey, Greece, Italy, Spain, France, Egypt, Lebanon, Palestine, Jordan, Israel, Mexico, the British Virgin Islands, the Bahamas, Chile, Brazil, and the Antarctica. His current research interests are in both cultural archaeology and in human behavior.

Author of many books, he is best known for his groundbreaking **Twelve Keys to an Effective Church**, which has formed the basis for the widely acclaimed Mission Growth Movement, which is helping many persons across the planet.

Dr. Callahan has earned B. A., M. Div., S. T. M., and Ph. D. degrees.

He has served as a pastor of rural and city congregations in Ohio, Texas, and Georgia.

He taught for many years at Emory University.

His recent book, **Living in Grace**, is helping many persons across the planet. Three recent books include the new edition of **Twelve Keys to an Effective Church,** the new edition of the **Twelve Keys Leaders' Guide,** and the new **Twelve Keys Bible Study.** Altogether, he is the author of twenty books.

Ken and Julie, his wife, celebrated being married for fifty-seven years on August 11, 2013. They have two sons, Ken, Jr., and Michael, and three grandsons: Blake, Mason, and Brice. They enjoy being with their family and their many good friends. They share good fun and good times with the outdoors, hiking, camping, reading, researching, traveling, quilting, and sailing. They enjoy being with one another.

Ken and Julie Callahan are visiting friends in the Shenandoah Valley of Virginia, enjoying the Blue Ridge Mountains with the Skyline Drive meandering along the ridges.

The picture is taken at the Rivers Bend Ranch of Elaine and Mac McConnell, outside of Stanley, Virginia. Ken and Julie are on the deck of Richard and Elizabeth Worden's Avion travel trailer on the Ranch.

Richard Worden, their long time, good friend, is taking the picture. Richard has written of Ken and Julie, "The history and beauty of the Valley grace their lives even as they have graced the lives of friends, colleagues and congregations for decades."

BOOKS BY KENNON L. CALLAHAN, PH.D.

Living in Peace   ISBN 978-1491088753

An encouraging, helpful book that shares possibilities for living in peace. Discover ten helpful events. Discover wonderful persons in Eunice, Mrs. Perkins, Gene, Charles, Ken, Opal, Grandma Ida and Kate, Mom, Mimi, Aunt Bea, St. John's, Dorothy, Grand Children, Orville, and Ken and Julie. Discover peace. Live in grace and peace.

Living in Grace   ISBN 978-1481200882

A joyful, encouraging book that shares possibilities for living in grace. Discover twelve decisive events. Discover remarkable persons of grace. Strengthen your living in grace. You will find this book helpful in your own life—living in grace.

Twelve Keys to an Effective Church: Strong, Healthy Congregations Living in the Grace of God, Second Edition   ISBN 978-0-470-55929-1

For the first time in print, the five basic qualities for strong, healthy congregations. New possibilities for an effective, successful congregation. New suggestions for expanding your current strengths and adding new strengths. New wisdom and insights on mission, sacrament, and grace. The book helps you to be a mission growth congregation.

The Twelve Keys Leaders' Guide: An Approach for Grassroots, Key Leaders, and Pastors Together   ISBN 978-0-470-55928-4

Lead your congregation in developing a strong, healthy future. Excellent ideas and good suggestions on how to lead a helpful *Twelve Keys* planning retreat. Resources for encouraging action, implementation, and momentum. Insights on the dynamics of memory, change, conflict, and hope in congregations. An excellent companion for the new *Twelve Keys* book.

The Twelve Keys Bible Study   ISBN 978-0-470-55916-1

Biblical resources for the *Twelve Keys*. Scriptures for each of the *Twelve Keys* and reflections on these scriptures. Suggestions and questions for study and conversation. Helpful for Advent and Lenten Bible studies, and for preaching and worship services. An excellent companion Bible study for the new *Twelve Keys* book.

The Future That Has Come   ISBN 0 7879 49817

The seven major paradigm shifts of recent years. New possibilities for reaching and growing the grassroots. Motivating and leading your congregation.

Small, Strong Congregations   ISBN 0 7879 49809

The distinctive dynamics of small, strong congregations. Ministers, leaders, and members of small congregations develop a strong, healthy future together.

A New Beginning for Pastors and Congregations   ISBN 0 7879 42898

What to do in the first three months of a new pastorate; how to make a new start in a present pastorate.

Preaching Grace   ISBN 0 7879 42952

Develop an approach to preaching that matches your own distinctive gifts. Help your preaching share the spirit of grace with your people,

Twelve Keys for Living   ISBN 0 7879 41409

Claim the strengths for living that God gives you. Develop a whole, healthy life. Solid Lenten or Advent study.

Visiting in an Age of Mission   ISBN 0 7879 38688

Develop shepherding in your congregation. Groupings to shepherd. The variety of ways you can shepherd.

Effective Church Finances   ISBN 0 7879 38696

Develop an effective budget, set solid giving goals, and increase the giving of your congregation.

Dynamic Worship   ISBN 0 7879 38661

Major resources for stirring, inspiring worship services, helpful and hopeful in advancing people's lives.

Giving and Stewardship   ISBN 0 7879 3867X

Grow generous givers. Motivations out of which people give. Six primary sources of giving. Giving principles in generous congregations. How to encourage your whole giving family.

Effective Church Leadership   ISBN 0 7879 38653

Foundational life searches. Seven best ways to grow leaders. Develop constructive leadership.

Building for Effective Mission   ISBN 0 7879 38726

Develop your mission. Evaluate locations. Maximize current facilities. Building new space. Create an effective building team. Selecting an architect. Develop an extraordinary first year.

Twelve Keys to an Effective Church   ISBN 0 7879 38718

Claim your current strengths, expand some, and add new strengths to be a strong, healthy congregation. Encourage your whole congregation to study this book—it helps in their church, family, work, and life.

Twelve Keys: The Planning Workbook   ISBN 0 7879 38734

Each person contributes directly to creating an effective long-range plan for your future together.

Twelve Keys: The Leaders' Guide   ISBN 0 7879 3870x

How to lead your congregation in developing an effective plan for your future. How to develop action, implementation, and momentum. Dealing with the dynamics of memory, change, conflict, and hope.

Twelve Keys: The Study Guide   ISBN 0 7879 39420

An excellent Bible study of the *Twelve Keys,* with helpful resources and solid discussion possibilities.

God bless you
with
grace and peace....

CPSIA information can be obtained at www.ICGtesting.com
Printed in the USA
LVOW11s1945091115

461719LV00001B/356/P